LEVEL 4

Written by: Caroline Laidlaw
Series Editor: Melanie Williams

Pearson Education Limited
Edinburgh Gate, Harlow,
Essex CM20 2JE, England
and Associated Companies throughout the world.

ISBN: 978-1-4082-8838-2

This edition first published by Pearson Education Ltd 2013
10
Text copyright © Pearson Education Ltd 2013

The moral rights of the author have been asserted
in accordance with the Copyright Designs and Patents Act 1988

Set in 17/21pt OT Fiendstar
Printed in Great Britain by Ashford Colour Press Ltd.
SWTC/01

Acknowledgements

The publisher would like to thank the following for their kind permission to reproduce their photographs:
(Key: b-bottom; c-centre; l-left; r-right; t-top)

Alamy Images: Arco Images GmbH 9t, Images of Africa Photobank 10-11, Juniors Bildarchiv GmbH 4b, kids Child Baby 23cl, Louise Heusinkveld 24c, Planet pix 15b, Steve Bloom Images 13; **Ardea:** Ferrero-Labat 24cr; **Corbis:** Frans Lanting 9b, Gerald Kooyman 18b, Kevin Schafer 14, moodboard 7, Ocean 9bl, Tim Clayton / 101010 23r; **Fotolia.com:** Kitch Bain 12b; **Getty Images:** Jeff Foott 24r, Mark Conlin 20t, Michael & Patricia Fogden 6, Sylvain Cordier 21t; **Photoshot Holdings Limited:** Bruce Coleman 8t, Juniors Tierbildarchiv 19, NHPA18tr; **Shutterstock.com:** Bumihills 12t, iDesign 16, Jason Patrick Ross 17b, Juriah Mosin 23c, Kjersti Joergensen 24l, max blain 23l, Nachiketa Bejaj 5t, photobar 5b, Sari O'Neal 3r, Vtldtlm 24cl; **SuperStock:** John Cancalosi / age fotostock 23cr
Cover images: Front: **Shutterstock.com:** palmenpep

All other images © Pearson Education

In some instances we have been unable to trace the owners of copyright material,
and we would appreciate any information that would enable us to do so.

Illustrations: Alan Rowe

For a complete list of the titles available in the Pearson English Kids Readers series, please go to www.pearsonenglishkidsreaders.com. Alternatively, write to your local Pearson Education office or to Pearson English Readers Marketing Department, Pearson Education, Edinburgh Gate, Harlow, Essex CM20 2JE, England.

Cool Cats

Cats live in towns, in villages and on farms. Do you sometimes watch cats? How do they move? They are good at running, climbing and jumping. They are champions. Cool cats practise being good athletes every day because they are predators. They must run faster than their prey, before they can catch it.

Fast mouse, faster cat!

Tigers and cheetahs are big cats. They do not live with people because they are wild animals. They live in forest habitats and grassland and where they can find big prey.

The tiger is the biggest of all the big cats. It lives in different countries of Asia. Because it swims well, it can carry its prey through water.

But I hate water!

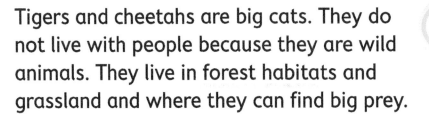

It is a dangerous predator because it runs very fast and can jump more than 4 metres. A tiger can easily hide in trees and long grass, where its prey cannot see it.

The cheetah is the fastest animal on four legs. It can run at a speed of 120 km/h. It is a champion athlete.

cheetah

Acrobats in Trees

Spider monkeys live in forest habitats in Central and South America. They have prehensile tails which hold on to branches. They can swing from branch to branch with their tails. At the same time they can hold food in their hands.

Spider monkeys eat plants, insects and birds' eggs. They are fantastic acrobats in trees.

Gibbons live
in forests of
Southeast Asia.
They have no tails
but they have long arms,
and long hands and feet.

These acrobats can swing
more than 10 metres between
trees, high above the ground.
They eat plants and insects.

Gibbons are the fastest animals
which live in trees. On the ground
they walk more slowly, on two legs.

Flying squirrels live in North American forests. They sleep in trees in the day. At night they fly down and find food.

How do they fly? They make the shape of two wings with their body, and glide. They can glide for 46 metres. That is fantastic for animals which have no wings.

I'm good at climbing up, but ...

Athletes on Land

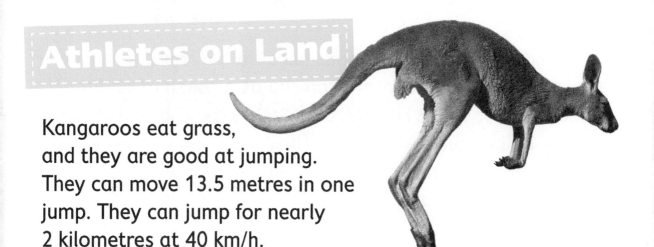

Kangaroos eat grass, and they are good at jumping. They can move 13.5 metres in one jump. They can jump for nearly 2 kilometres at 40 km/h.

The red kangaroo lives in the driest parts of Australia, where there is not much grass. The red kangaroo often has to jump a long way before it finds food.

African wild dogs are famous because they have fantastic stamina. These predators can run at a speed of about 56 km/h for 5 or 6 kilometres. Because they have stamina they do not get tired quickly. Their prey usually runs faster, but then it becomes tired and weak. It cannot run any longer and the dogs kill it.

African wild dog

African wild dogs catch gazelles, but these animals are difficult prey. They can run at a speed of 80 km/h. They can also jump in the air and run at the same time. The dogs kill only the weakest and youngest gazelles.

African wild dogs and gazelles are long-distance athletes. They can run a long way before they get tired.

gazelle

Asian and West African elephants live in jungle habitats. Some of these animals work for people, because they can lift and carry heavy things.

All elephants have stamina for long-distance walking, but not for running.

In the east and south of Africa their grassland habitats are often dry for many months. The elephants must go a long way before they find grass and water. Hungry elephants can walk more than 30 kilometres in one day. They never forget places where there is water. They can drink about 200 litres every day, and eat 100 kilograms of food.

Athletes in the Air

Every autumn many storks leave Europe and fly south to Africa. They fly hundreds of kilometres. On the journey, they stop and find food. Then they take off again. The sun shines on the land, and warm air rises.

The birds begin flying and then they glide on rising air. They can glide for many kilometres. They fly back to Europe in spring, after the African winter.

The long-distance journeys of storks and Monarch butterflies

Birds are not the only long-distance athletes in the air. Every autumn, millions of Monarch butterflies fly south from their summer homes in North America. They fly thousands of kilometres to California and Mexico. In spring they fly north again.

A lot of butterflies die on this difficult journey.

Hummingbirds live in North, Central and South America. Why are they always flying round flowers? Because inside flowers there is nectar, which is their favourite food.

A hummingbird moves very quickly from flower to flower. It flies up, down and round. It is the only bird which can fly backwards. It is a champion acrobat in the air.

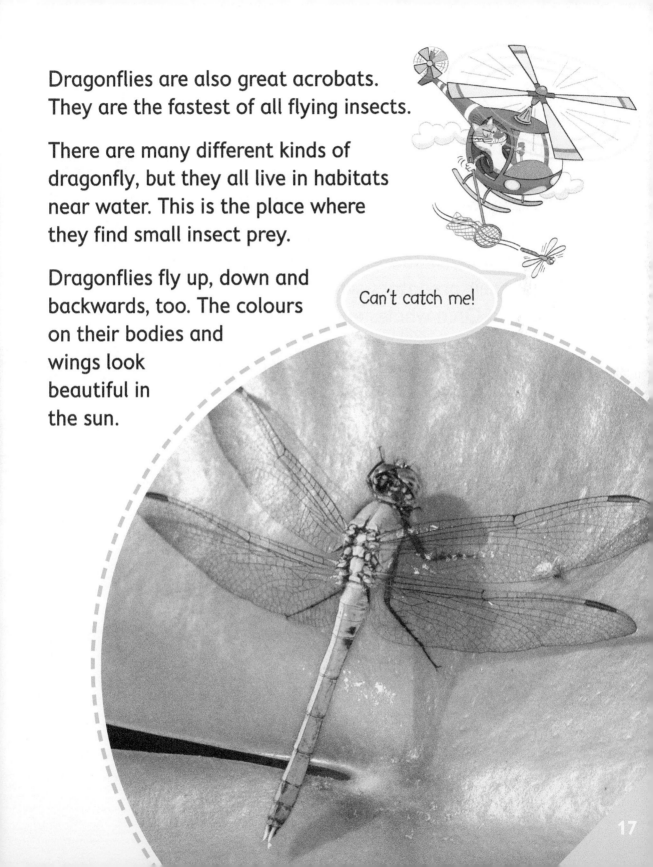

Dragonflies are also great acrobats. They are the fastest of all flying insects.

There are many different kinds of dragonfly, but they all live in habitats near water. This is the place where they find small insect prey.

Dragonflies fly up, down and backwards, too. The colours on their bodies and wings look beautiful in the sun.

Can't catch me!

Athletes in Water

Penguins live in Antarctica. They are birds, but they cannot fly. They move slowly on land where they walk and hop. In the sea they swim very fast. This is important because they catch fish there, and fish move fast. It is also important because their predators swim fast, too. Great white sharks and Orca whales eat penguins.

Dolphins are good acrobats, and like having fun. They enjoy swimming fast and jumping high in the water.

Dolphins are intelligent and friendly animals. They sometimes swim near ships and people enjoy watching them. Perhaps dolphins also like watching people. Perhaps they are saying to their friends, 'Look at those animals on legs! They're very slow.'

Alaska

USA

—— winter journey

—— summer journey

Mexico

The long-distance journeys of Grey whales

Grey whales are fantastic long-distance athletes. They live near Alaska in summer, where there is a lot of food. In winter they swim to warmer water near Mexico. They go there because there is better food. It is also the place where their babies are born. Later the whales swim back to Alaska. This is a journey of 20,000 kilometres.

Flying fish can jump out of the sea and glide two hundred metres. Their predators swim fast but they cannot fly. Are flying fish the best athletes?

Cheetahs are fastest on land and gibbons are fastest in trees. The best long-distance champions are whales. The fastest flying insects are dragonflies. And the best athletes? Cool cats!

What do you think?

Glossary

acrobat (n) page 6 — a person (or animal) who can swing, climb and move in different ways

athlete (n) page 3 — a person (or animal) who, for example, is very good at running, swimming, jumping

backwards (adv) page 16 — This boy is walking backwards.

branch (n) page 6 — part of a tree

glide (v) page 8 — a way of moving in the air

grassland (n) page 4 — a place where grass grows. It is often flat.

habitat (n) page 4 — a place where an animal lives

insect (n) page 6 — a small animal which has three pairs of legs, and usually two pairs of wings

long-distance (adj) page 11 — going a long way

nectar (n) page 16 — a plant food which is inside flowers

km/h page 5 — kilometres per hour

predator (n) page 3 — an animal which kills and eats animals for food

prehensile (tail) (adj) page 6 — part of an animal which can hold on to something

prey (n) page 3 — an animal which a predator kills and eats

stamina (n) page 10 — An animal has stamina because it can fly, walk, run or swim for a long time before it is tired.

Activity page ❶

Before You Read

1 **Look at the pictures.**

a Which activities can **you** do?

b Which activities can animals and birds do?

jump　　　　climb　　　　swim　　　　run　　　ride a bicycle

2 **Look in the book and find**

a an animal which only lives in water.

b an animal which only eats plant food.

c an animal which has beautiful colours on its body.

d an animal which is bigger than an elephant.

e an animal which runs very fast.

f an animal which you can see in your country.

After You Read

❶ Say or write the names of the animals. For example phantele = elephant. Then match the words and pictures.

a gerti   **b** act   **c** obbing   **d** lewha   **e** torks

❷ Who am I?

a I'm good at swinging in trees.

b I can swim and I can fly, but I am not a bird.

c I'm a predator. I can swim, and climb trees.

d I have two wings, and I can fly backwards.

e I have four wings, and I can fly thousands of kilometres.

f I live in the sea, and I can jump high out of the water.

❸ Read and write True (T) or False (F).

a A flying squirrel lives in grassland.

b A humming bird lives in places where there are flowers.

c A kangaroo lives in cold places where there is snow and ice.

d A gibbon lives in towns.

e A whale lives in the ocean.

f A stork flies to a different habitat in winter.